T0362800

1

© Knowledge Books and Software

There is a lot of life in the desert.

© Knowledge Books and Software

3

© Knowledge Books and Software

Big animals lived in the desert.
This is an emu.

© Knowledge Books and Software

5

© Knowledge Books and Software

Sand dunes had plants and animals.

© Knowledge Books and Software

7

© Knowledge Books and Software

The bilby lived in the sand dunes.

© Knowledge Books and Software

9

© Knowledge Books and Software

The thorny lizard lived below the sand.

© Knowledge Books and Software

11

© Knowledge Books and Software

The First People lived across all deserts.

© Knowledge Books and Software

13

© Knowledge Books and Software

Some food plants grow in the desert.

© Knowledge Books and Software

15

© Knowledge Books and Software

First People mob would look for food.

© Knowledge Books and Software

17

© Knowledge Books and Software

The desert had food for the First
People.

© Knowledge Books and Software

19

© Knowledge Books and Software

Grass seeds were ground up.
Flour was made for food.

© Knowledge Books and Software

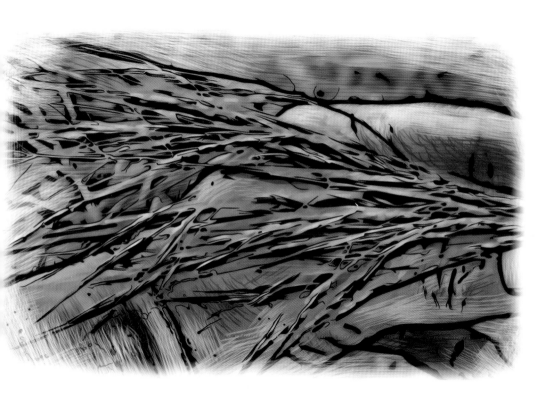

21

© Knowledge Books and Software

After a person dies - they will cry
and be sad together.

© Knowledge Books and Software

23

© Knowledge Books and Software

Word bank

desert

emu

plants

animals

sand

dunes

thorny

lizard

across

grow

grass

ceremonies

person

together

flour

© Knowledge Books and Software